Also by Shane McCrae

Sometimes I Never Suffered

The Gilded Auction Block

In the Language of My Captor

The Animal Too Big to Kill

Forgiveness Forgiveness

Blood

Mule

Cain Named the Animal

Farrar, Straus and Giroux

New York

Cain Named the Animal

Shane McCrae

Farrar, Straus and Giroux
120 Broadway, New York 10271

Printed in the United States of America
First edition, 2022

Library of Congress Cataloging-in-Publication Data
Names: McCrae, Shane, 1975– author.
Title: Cain named the animal / Shane McCrae.
Description: First edition. | New York : Farrar, Straus and Giroux, 2022.
Identifiers: LCCN 2021052086 | ISBN 9780374602857 (hardcover)
Subjects: LCGFT: Poetry.
Classification: LCC PS3613.C385747 C35 2022 | DDC 811/.6—dc23
LC record available at https://lccn.loc.gov/2021052086

Designed by Crisis

Our books may be purchased in bulk for promotional,
educational, or business use. Please contact your local
bookseller or the Macmillan Corporate and Premium Sales
Department at 1-800-221-7945, extension 5442, or by
email at MacmillanSpecialMarkets@macmillan.com.

www.fsgbooks.com
www.twitter.com/fsgbooks
www.facebook.com/fsgbooks

10 9 8 7 6 5 4 3 2 1

For my family, and for Taso

Do some people imagine themselves
in the same relation to their place of birth as a scab to a wound?

—Will Harris

Contents

Some Heavens Are All Silence   **3**

Love Poems and Others

Arm in the Excavator's Shovel   **7**

Whom I Have Blocked Out   **9**

To Make a Wound   **11**

A Letter to Lucie About Lucie   **12**

Worldful   **14**

To My Mother's Father   **17**

The King of the Sadnesses of Dogs   **18**

Eurydice on the Art of Poetry   **20**

Husbands   **22**

For Melissa Asleep Upstairs   **23**

Nowhere Is Local   **24**

The Professor   **25**

The Butterflies the Mountain and the Lake   **26**

For Sylvia Twenty-Eight in July   **27**

To Nicholas from My Absence   **28**

Having Been Raised by My Kidnappers I Consider the Gift of Life, or A Gift from a Thief   **29**

A Thousand Pictures   **30**

Please Come Flying   **32**

Vivian Maier Considers Heaven from a Bench in Rogers Beach Park Chicago   **33**

Recapitulations

The Hastily Assembled Angel on Embodiment   37

Jim Limber on Silence   39

Cain Named the Animal

The Lost Tribe of Eden   43

Constantly Throwing Up   44

The Lost Tribe of Eden at the Beginning of the Days of Blood   47

The Robot Bird Tells Me How It Is I Am in Hell   49

The Beginning of Time   53

The Reformation   56

In Which the Beginning of Time Happens in a Different Way   65

The Dream at the End of the Dream   68

Notes   81

Acknowledgments   83

Cain Named the Animal

Some Heavens Are All Silence

Listen to my last breath   you'll hear each breath I've drawn
Since my voice changed and the sound got
Deeper bow your head   pull down   a shroud from the heaven white
Folks get peace   privacy from pull one down

To cover us I know you got   a ladder or a string
A ladder in your pocket straight
And tall   a white string made of white strings twisted tight
Together and it hangs

Above your head you   pull and
A ladder rolls   down from that heaven
White folks pull grave by grave to Earth

I know y'all got a heaven   just for y'all and
A God who don't speak   or don't make y'all listen   listen
Bow your head   that is the voice of God   that breath

Love Poems and Others

Arm in the Excavator's Shovel

The excavation ripples through the body
The skeleton in dirt the   dirt at certain
Depths relative   to the skeleton corre-
    sponds to the shape   of the living person

Thus anyone   with the right coordinates
Could dig the shape of the person from the dirt
But made of dirt   but with his skeleton
    Inside it would it   be an *it*

When cradled   in the living arms of the worker
Because no   excavator has yet been
Designed to fear the thing it rips from the dirt
    No excavator   would be gen-

tle enough not to break the simula-
crum from its bone original and frame
Or would the crumbling shape   become a *him*
    The excavator tears an arm

Off   and it dangles from the shovel as
Clumps of dirt fall through the shovel's teeth meat   cooked
From the bone   the shovel raised to the sky   a mouth
    Gaping forever   and a sac-

rificial altar if   one's *it* the other

Must be *him*   a worker waves her arms

The skull at her feet   but who does not praise

　　The mouth to whom the body comes

Whom I Have Blocked Out

Asked *Have you ever* asked   *ridden a horse before*   / Said
He's real gentle   and lifted me up

I trusted what men said was gentle
to hurt   and I knew I couldn't say / *No*

to what men said was gentle
and lifted me up

    *   *   *

Onto the horse no   saddle he
Without a saddle seemed   naked the horse seemed more

Naked than I could make myself naked
but not   / As naked as I could be made to be   / Lifted

me up from the day / At the farm
Into the memory already forming

    *   *   *

Me crouched low trembling clinging to the mane
The mane   alive but not as part / Of the body of the horse alive

As part of the wind a fire at the end of the wind
Me burning in it six   years old by six

I have / Already been   / A sickness in the hearts of men
By six I've been the sieve through

     *   *   *

Which they expel their sickness
said / *You ever*

ridden said the man   who must have been
the father of the friend / From school who had invited me to the farm

And this is how I have forgiven him   / I have remembered
only the beginning of the ride

     *   *   *

Then nothing then the bath   in the trough in the field
Far from the house in the brown water stripping in / The field

your body is a gift you have to live through
Remember me my suffering to me

To whom   have I been suffering
To whom will I be healed

To Make a Wound

I roll two sheets in   like you taught me so
The platen won't get worn out   and again
I write to you   I write you here   I know
Now you're more me than you   I'm writing in

Winter and you're the stiffness and the cold
Still in my fingers   but in summer you
Would be   the bladed fingers wounding cold
Air from the hot   air at the window you

Would be   the roaring of the blades
Hacking the summer from the air   and my relief
Grandmother tell me is it best to breathe
But is it better to be comforted

We didn't speak for years   after I left
Writing you here I give the death I take
I know I should feel wounded by your death
I write to you to make a wound write back

A Letter to Lucie About Lucie

She gave it with her living hand to me a copy of
    The Master Letters with her living hand to me
Thick with a thickness they now   I can't say   how many re-
    printings later new   copies have lost the paper
They're printed on is thinner   now but it itself was new
    She gave it to me new she must have had it since
The book was new to her she must have   kept it in her castle
    She signed it   *in the Little Castle* that was where we were

Together she   you must have kept it in your castle for
    Twenty years Master how   long had you lived in the castle
Before I for a single afternoon   came where are you
    To ask   I think   the castle followed you   your whole life
And now you've taken the castle   to wherever you have gone
    Master of now   gone from now
                                 she must have kept that
Copy for twenty years before   she with her living hand
    Gave it to me   a paperback   still glossy with

The printing date *4/97* still   glossy beneath
    The gloss or Master was it   printed *on* the gloss
As we are we who   walk on Earth are   printed on the gloss
    And liable to smudge and   disappear if touched

I ask you where are you to ask   I might have   called you after
    I heard   but first I'll tell the story   we were under-
ground waiting for a train my daughter and   I waiting for
    An A or D   to ride it down   to Union Square when

I heard a woman go   under the train   and the sound must
    Have been the train   crushing her body but the sound sounded
Like a piece of paper tearing that was   what it sounded
    Like   then screaming and the screaming was the sound
I turned to   Master then I turned my daughter's face away
    I might have called you after   I might have said *It sounded*
Like paper Master where are you to ask   do you know now to
    Whom she was Master   the woman beneath the train

You must have kept it   in your little castle not for   me in
    Particular   but for whoever would be there calling
You when your love was called   to cross the bridge from hand to hand
    The book would for a moment make as it was given
And I was there   I called you and you   with your living hand
    Took the book down from the shelf   beside the sprig of heather
From the Brontës' moors   and handed it to me   a sprig that looked
    Alive still   of green heather   from across the sea

Worldful

In down some part of me I hadn't noticed
Before in down   but not dark   bright
Today I saw a nothingness   outlined in white
Shaped like a kidney-shaped   swimming pool floating

Above a landscape like a California
Postcard all pastel   blues and tans and green
With unimaginable life or life that
Would have to be reduced to be imagined

And seeing it I knew it was   the nothingness
An image of a feeling of   me feeling still
Dependent on my grandparents a feel-
ing like at any   moment I could just

Call them and ask for help with food with rent my grand-
mother is dead   and has been dead for fourteen
Years calculating the   number just now
I thought it might have been   two   years I thought

It might have been   even though I knew
Two years I thought   worldful gone twice
Of sun and night   since my   grandmother left the
Sun and the night   for the unmeasured world

It might have been two   and I haven't spo-
ken to   my grandfather for twenty-eight
Years and I don't know   but I think he might
Be dead too   or alive in Arizo-

na yesterday   I saw him on the 1
Uptown from 34th   Street he was sitting
Across from someone I had never
Seen before   and she was saying something

Serious to him and he was trying   to keep up
And he couldn't   his face was
A wrinkled gray suit hanging from his face
And he was wearing a gray suit   he kept

Glancing at the briefcase at his feet then looking
Up at the woman like   a dog afraid
It will be beaten he   who always hit
Me harder than I could have hit him back

If I had thought I could have hit him back
And lived I wanted to   rise from my seat
And throw   my arms around him and to not
Remember why I want to never   speak

To him again   I wanted to and then
Remembered why I want to never   touch
Him or be touched by him   again instead I watched
Him and the woman her face softening

As he began   and whisperingly failed
To and began again to answer a
Question I hadn't heard   but what life does
Not have to be reduced to be imagined

To My Mother's Father

Our sorrow and our love move into a foreign language.
—C. P. Cavafy (tr. by Edmund Keeley and Philip Sherrard)

English is dead   even though you still say English
Words even though you still   put them in English order
Your English is dead   yet it tugs away from you
Like a strong dog fighting a leash   the harder

It fights the   greater is your fear
It won't if it gets free   return En-
glish fights you like a language   you're
Taking in school   knowing you'll never see the country

In the spring the trees outside the window are
Alive with life in the fall alive
With death   all year the teacher's voice slips past you
A distant ambulance in a strange city

English is dead   the one Great Dane you've ev-
er seen in real life howls in the street   still but its howl is
Noise to you now now   you don't recognize
The feeling in its cry   its foreign vowels

The King of the Sadnesses of Dogs

1.

I brought my gift to the king of the sadnesses of dogs
He sighed the sigh he sighs   in the stories children read
The sigh that makes the dogs of the kingdom howl   no matter
How far from the king the dogs might rest   their noisy heads

I set my gift on   one of the stacks   at the foot of the steps
By which one mounts from the long blue gold-fringed rug   to the foot
Of the throne of the king I walked   the length of the hall beside
The rug upon which none but the king walks   and set

My gift on top of the stack   then bowed and backed away
The throne looked chiseled from a single stone the color
Of yellowed bone   and flecked with brown like meat and blood
Clinging to bone   the stain and spread of them being yellow

He sighed the sigh he sighs   and close disharmonies
Filled the grand hall   as if an organist had pressed
Down all the keys   of a pipe organ bigger than
The hall itself the stampede   of dogs' sadnesses

Rattled the men in the stained glass   in the high windows
At which the sunlight stopped   through which it could not pass

Sadnesses crowded so against the glass   I tripped and
Fell and was pinned by the howls   flat on my back   on the glass-

y stones beside the rug

2.

                    I saw myself a man-
Sized beetle writhing on the glassy green and white
Stones my arms flapping my green   body twisting   bucking
To free itself of the vision by enacting it

Trapped by its struggle to get free   I saw myself
And saw   the gold I weeks before had scooped from the stream
Beside my shanty   in my hand in the small water
Cupped in my hand   and saw the thin ring I had ham-

mered from the gold   sunken in the glass box   I had bor-
rowed from my neighbor   knowing I never would return it
I saw myself   writhing on the stones   wearing the finest suit my
Neighbor would lend me   and I saw myself   still   sending

It back by courier from the palace   in a burlap
Sack stamped with the king's seal   while the howls shook the stones
As if they were an army stamping on the stones
I writhed and trembled hoping   still on the trembling stones

Eurydice on the Art of Poetry

The story you have   heard is false   it's true
He sang for me   and true he lulled the god
Who didn't care to fight him   easily
The god is like us all   the blood of the dead

Is made wine by their sorrow some   don't argue
And others never stop   I followed him
Yes but he wasn't   told he couldn't look
He didn't look because he felt ashamed

I know now he already had the poem
Finished or nearly   so before he left
For the underworld   he didn't come for me
He came to check the details   he had thought

He'd fail to win me back   and in the end
Yes   at the mouth of the cave he just ran off
I think he didn't know what else to do
I didn't follow him   it was a relief

To be allowed to keep my death   I heard
The poem first in the spring   sung by a new-

ly murdered boy who didn't know my name
When he was told my name   why should he have

I wasn't in the poem   the poem was true

Husbands

My house, my bed, my husbands
—Savages

O dream   I live in which I dream
Whose dreams   I have and failing tried
Not harming them to live inside
Too often making   like a pet dog sudden-
ly unfamiliar killing a wild rabbit en-
raged for no reason he   even with the body
Between his red teeth knows   subsum-
ing the wild blood and body   too often making your dreams mine

And leaves his wildness after   and returns
To his old self   but now for anyone
Who saw him wild the blood now   stains his mouth
Forever   for anyone   who saw the rabbit move
Still   like it was alive still   moving with
The motion of the jaws consuming it

For Melissa Asleep Upstairs

Midwinter spring a mouse since we
Have risen   some from poverty
It's not a rat flies everywhere
Above my head   below your bod-
y in the ceiling in the floor
I pick its shit from the countertop
And later don't say anything
The only part of my mind not
Flying in your talk then   being the part
That keeps the shit from you   false spring
Undecorates the eaves and boughs
The animals can't find their season
Though it is everywhere now   life fills even
The shadows in our house

Nowhere Is Local

Ten years and we to New York now
Have moved from Iowa to from Ohio how   far from New York
To anywhere now I don't know
But everywhere seems here or visits and   nowhere is local

I've never anywhere I've
Lived before wanted to be buried where I've lived
But have ignored live-
long all my life the longest part of life

From fear or fear   of the diminishment
Of love or of   love from the diminishing of joy
But greet it here with you the longest part

Of life it   can be is a joy to want
To be dead somewhere   is a joy to rest the heart
Let me die here where I don't want to die

The Professor

The air is colder than the light in the air
No fog   no smoke   but the light hangs on the air
Like fog   like smoke   I'm walking to the bakery
On Amsterdam   across from the cathedral

A middle-aged   man wearing a tweed cap and
A limp blue Members Only jacket passes me
And a black face mask with a white skull
Printed on it   but death is a professor everywhere

What have you learned he asks
What do you know
I turn the corner and the sidewalk's full of stu-
dents   everybody's parents sent them hoping

Back   elsewhere   the professor hangs his jacket on his chair
Sighs off his cap   tightens his mask

The Butterflies the Mountain and the Lake

It's Saturday   most often neighbor   we
Are walking with our daughter lately   even when / We walk together
everywhere we go we want to go home everywhere   / But oh
hey did you see that story

about the butterflies the mountain and the lake
the   / Butterflies monarch butterflies huge swarms they
Migrate and as they migrate south   as they
Cross Lake Superior instead of flying

South straight across they fly
South over the water then fly east
still over the water then fly south   again / And now
biologists believe they   turn to avoid a mountain

That disappeared millennia ago   / No
butterfly lives long enough to fly   the whole migration
From the beginning to the end
they / Lay eggs along the way

Just as you and I   most often neighbor
Migrate together in our daughter   over a dark lake
We make with joy the child we make
And mountains are reborn in her

For Sylvia Twenty-Eight in July

You're three and I can see you you have run away
  Across the park you turned once   first you ran
  Fifteen or twenty steps or only ten
Laughing then turned to make   sure I was watching you

Still in the boxed-in   park in the empty park in   Salem where
  We live   except for some tall evergreens
  With wide and bare trunks   near the library
And then you ran until you were half hidden   far-

ther   you're hiding behind a tree   I see your arm
  The branches meet above your head in the branches
  And part in sudden gusts   you shout *Come find me*
You're three you're young enough   to go and not be gone

To Nicholas from My Absence

You are now you have been   you are now seventeen
When I was seventeen I had the
Year before met my father
Whom I had known before   but I had been

Kidnapped for thirteen years and thousands
Of miles away   in nowhere he would think to look for me
But I know where you are and we
Know where we are I send you   texts and you send

Texts back from fewer thousands of
Miles from it's Maps I just   checked says it's fifteen hundred miles
Away   from fifteen hundred miles away

When I was seventeen I couldn't love
My father like his child
Whom I had been when I was three   I am a blank where I should be

Having Been Raised by My Kidnappers I
Consider the Gift of Life, or A Gift from a Thief

A gift that disappears as it is given
A gift from whom whenever   they give you anything
You have to ask them where they got it from
A gift that disappears and takes you with it

A gift for which you will not be forgiven
Whether you give it or receive it when
My mother's parents kidnapped me   my grand-
mother said I would see my father

Again in a few days   and the big wheel he
Had given me   the gift
She gave me then   and then   for thirteen years

I didn't   you must close your eyes   for the gift
After you open it it's   stolen   but it wasn't stolen
For you   no one will give you who you are

A Thousand Pictures

A picture says a picture
is only a picture of   / Not what the picture is
a picture of

But what it's for a   picture is a picture
of the future   even when
You're older and you can't remember

The trip you can't remember
anybody   / Else on the team and what position
did you play

What   were you eating you
can't tell   / Even though you see a / Red flake
of pepper   or blood on your fork

Even though you see your face
You're not sure now
whether you were afraid   / Of the deer eating

from your hand and was your hand / Empty
you don't see any food in the picture
And was somebody

whispering   / *Hold out your hand* / Who
was whispering   / Who took the picture who
could tell you now

Who knows enough   about your life to
Give your life back to you
A picture says

your life has no beginning
A thousand pictures say your life
will end a thousand times

Please Come Flying

Lucie I'm flying south to you
    Through winter on a train
You beat the summer one last time
My body takes me where I go

Bearing my thousand single love for
    You   now that you can't hear me
Quietly   to the cemetery
The long train knocks   the long train shivers

Beneath the weight   I shiver most
    Beside me   fast rain fills the
Window   displacing as it spills a-
cross the glass   light   I staring west

Mistake light leaving for light dying
    Lucie as the light flies
Sparkling from the glass   back to the sky
In raindrops flying   that fall back flying

Vivian Maier Considers Heaven from a
Bench in Rogers Beach Park Chicago

In Heaven nobody will be alone
In Heaven   except for me and nobody
   Nobody calls   nobody comes
My nobody expands across the country

The way a parachute expands across
The sky   it does if you're right under it
   In Heaven they'll throw me   in the lost
And found   where I guess everybody goes

At first   now   that I think about it   what
Will be my special place apart   I wonder
   Or will they leave me in the lost
And found box after they have scooped the heaven-

ly out   a permanent person in a tem
porary place   roles are reversed in Heaven
   Nobody calls   nobody comes
In Heaven I expect the children are

A kind of furniture   nobody sits on
Like flowers in Manhattan   maybe sometimes

They're brought to God and God says *This one*
And that   ottoman is sent back to life

A baby   and for some this seems to never
Happen   I think I'm such a child returned
    Most things in my life seemed to never
Happen before they happened   now they seem to

Have never happened though they have   for the time
Being I am   for now I'm stuck in most
    Things having never happened I'm
A lamp   shining in an abandoned building

But for a lamp I think that would be Heaven

Recapitulations

The Hastily Assembled Angel on Embodiment

The hastily assembled angel's sure he never
Before he had a body had a body
How could he have   though he   thinks he remembers
Watching the other angels build him from above the

Parts they were hammering together were
Folding together stapling   together paper-
clipping together nobody   yet living where
Staples and paper clips would come from paper

To fold   but hammers always were and things
To strike bodies   to strike except for his
Which he's sure   could not have been
Before it was   but he recalls an eminence

As if he once had been a spotlight's beam
Shining from somewhere in a medium-sized
City   untraceable and from
Which the place takes its mystery   to whom does

The spotlight call   and from where does it call
And does the pillar of light emanate
From the shadowy machine beaming   from tall
Grass or a parking lot   amidst low-mileage late-

Model used cars   or does the pillar of
Light emanate instead from the heaven
It brightens and does not explain   the oth-
er angels when they built him

Built him so hurriedly he never had the
Chance to ask them questions   not
Good questions not   the questions anybody
Might as they watched their body built beneath them   ask like *What*

Is happening he   thinks he might have asked
Like *Help*   he thinks he might have asked *Why am I*
So high why can't I kneel and make
With you whatever you're   *making* the hastily assembled

Angel is sure   he saw the tops of the other an-
gels' heads before he saw their bodies
Before he saw their hands
Shaking like the hands of humans when   humans are pleading

Though at the time he knew
Nothing he could compare the shaking to

Jim Limber on Silence

I reckon I'm the youngest one of me
I mean I died the youngest what I mean
Is I'm the youngest me who talks   I died when I was three
But woke in Heaven grown I've seen   the younger ones through
    the win-

dows in the Room of Watching Heavens Heaven
Is many Heavens   one for each person
A person might have been each   Heaven is different
But I've seen more than

One where no Negro ever was a slave
And many where I died   in infancy
They're grown like me   but I have nev-
er heard them speak   but I have seen those Negroes see-

ing Heaven   like it's their native world
And each of their black faces is a song of words

Cain Named the Animal

The Lost Tribe of Eden

They knew they'd disappear they knew the stars
And sun shone for the naked pair they knew
Not to complain   they knew they couldn't choose the prayer
God finally would answer to

What if it was no prayer   they knew the fields
Outside the garden were alive and growing
They knew to fear   they knew God hadn't said
Enough about the tree they knew   the use of knowing

They knew the angels knew the will of God
They knew the angels whispered late at night
They knew the fruit they knew   the apple

Wept in their mouths   when bitten   like a good
Smell on the serpent's tongue   him they knew best
On his long legs he stood as tall as people

Constantly Throwing Up

    I thought the bird would leave I thought
    The bird would leave abandon me
And as the human voice inside the bird wound
    Down slowed   down like a record slowing
    Down it got deeper as it slowed
But also   louder and the old west buildings
    Surrounding me   shook and the voice
    Got so loud I had to cover
My ears and finally the buildings   popped
    And disappeared   like how soap bubbles
    In cartoons pop   like how they van-
ish in a flash of white they vanish in-
    to the center of where they used
    To be   except the old west buildings
Vanished into blood   the buildings popped
    And left red flashes of what looked like
    Blood hanging in the air   blood aster-
isks hanging in the air   the bird looked restless

    And shook its feathers   absently
    At first   then desperately   as if
They were a coat a spider had just crawled in-
    to glancing from its wings to me

And back   repeatedly as the
Human voice inside its chest grew louder
   More quickly as the voice grew louder
   Until the buildings popped   and then the
Bird closed its beak   and turned to fly away but
   Crouching to leap   turned back to me
   And barked *Hey   dumbfuck do you really*
Get   what's happened to you do you know you're
   In Hell   'cause I don't think you do you
   Look like a dad on   his first campus
Tour   no   you don't know   do you at least feel your
   Feet getting heavy I   see it please
   Tell me you fucking feel it I
Looked   down   and saw blue roots   had sprouted through

   The swooshes on my shoes   and into
   The dark red dirt I   jumped   the roots
Stretched and snapped *Won't   be so easy next time*
   Fuckface you know what   I should just
   Leave like I never saw you just
Let you fucking   root you helpless shit   shit
   SHIT   c'mon asshole   follow me   it
   Growled those last few words   through its beak
Its beak   was perforated like a strainer
   And metal like a strainer not the
   Mesh kind a steel bowl pounded flat
Punctured then hammered cold   into a funnel

Oil   spluttered constantly from the holes

As if the bird were throwing up

Constantly in its beak   and later I

Learned   it was   that's what   makes Hell *Hell*

You can't escape what you consume

You must take part in the suffering that feeds you

The Lost Tribe of Eden at the
Beginning of the Days of Blood

Each night the trees   at the edges of the garden
     Stretched   close together and the slender branches
Of each tree intertwined with the slender branch-
     es of its neighbor   and the leaves of one en-
folded the leaves of the other and the trees
     Together made a wall and partial roof
The people of   the tribe of Eden saw
     The colors of the Milky Way above
Them if they looked directly up if they
     Leaned so far back they   almost lost their bal-
ance tilting   their heads back to the edge of falling
     But if they looked ahead and up   the wall
Blocked what they all imagined were more stars
     From the moment the first stars appeared each night

—

At the horizons God   rehearsed the world
     Struggling especially to get time right
And held the night and colors in the sky
     Above the garden wheeling   days around
It like a whirlwind one   the next   the next
     Each bloodier than the day before it end-

less blood   but fitting in a finite space
     Of time   but how   God first thought time itself
Was flawed   but time was God's first mirror   as
     Impossible and simple as themselves
Almost   it was flawless   almost no the flaw from
     Which blood poured endlessly   had to be some-
thing else and God reset the days again
     And spun them forward and reset and spun
Them and for generations of the tribe
     Of Eden God rehearsed the world   until
One night a boy   who hoped to see the sky
     Beyond the edges of the visible
Climbed one of the trees in the wall of trees the tree
     Though it had stretched   to stop the tribe from seeing
The sky at the horizon stood
     Still and it was a tree   a boy was climbing being
A tree and the boy climbed   quickly through the can-
     opy and saw   the whirling days and saw
Faces like his   in the days and faces like
     No faces he had ever seen   and raw
Incomprehensible machines   and blood
     None in the tribe had seen   blood before even
The happiness he saw looked strange to him
     Shadowed as if   with the shadows at the edges
Of the wall   the stunned   boy lost his balance and
     Fell   through the canopy to the garden floor
And broke his bones and bones   broke through his skin
     The boy's blood glistened on the rocks and flowers

The Robot Bird Tells Me How It Is I Am in Hell

My name is Law   I do the work
The boss says he   created me in
The   in the however long it was
Between when Cain crushed Abel's fore-

head with a rock   and the first drop of
Blood hit the ground   I was the voice
Of the blood crying out to God
You know   the thing in the Bible   God says

The voice of thy   brother's blood crieth
Unto me from the ground *that shit*
Happened   I was a baby all fucking
Bawling and shit   yeah   anyway

I say that makes   Cain killing Abel
I say that makes   Abel poor dickless
Abel the   first human and
The father of all humankind

But the boss he says different
He says it's him   the boss   for making
The murder possible and he's
Not   philosophical like me

He doesn't have to be but he
Is sure as shit he's   fucking   he's
Smarter than me   smarter than you
Anyway so   listen   a couple

Weeks ago we got a fax
You think there'd be   a phone in Hell
Fuck no   we fax   so anyway
We got a fax   about you shit-

For-brains it said you   would be coming
Down and the boss wanted you
To get a tour   at first I thought
It meant the boss down here because   you

Know   he's the boss I think things mean
But then I heard him   shouting and
Breaking shit   in the throne room and
I realized   it meant the boss boss

And as this dawns on me he   stomps
Out of the throne room sees the I
Don't know the joy of knowing what's
Going on for once flash in my eyes

Or some shit and he's fucking pissed
Next thing I know I'm guiding your

Slow ass through Hell   but the boss doesn't
Want you to know you're getting special

Treatment so if you see him   keep your
Mouth shut oh shit   how will you breathe
Don't look at me like that I know you're
Not breathing   it still works   so anyway

Back to Abel   what I think is
If Abel's not your father Cain
Is after   all he had the big
Rock   and how many times you think

He saw his dad kill anything by
Crushing its head not   many right
Nah man an arrow in the heart
And by the way that's what God gave you

By telling Adam he could name
The animals   God told you where
Their hearts were   Adam never missed a
Shot   you might think   this sounds like bullshit

But he was using a gift God
Had given him   so killing was
Like prayer for him   but Cain   he looked
Abel in the eyes   and saw himself

Not in his brother's heart   but in
His head   and crushed his head   and yeah
Where else do humans start   Cain named
The animal in Abel's head

The Beginning of Time

1. The Lost Tribe of Eden and the Word

The tribe of Eden watching watched time
Enter the garden what they saw
A sky-wide lake a shallow pale
Blue paler than the sky was blue

But flowing like a river but
A circle not a line   but flow-
ing like a lizard flowing in
The cage of a child's hands   although

They had no word for *cage*   time floated
In the air above them   like a glass cloud
Between them and the sky although
They had no word for *glass*   a glass cloche

Lowered from far behind the sky in-
to place   between them and the sky
Although they had no word for *cloche*
And from the cloche the cloud a sky

That wasn't the blue sky behind
The glass a layer of the un-

derside of the glass   peeled from the glass
And fell and falling melted in

The air and melting either clung
To everything and everyone
In the garden or evaporated
Completely   no one in the tribe knew

This happened years before the man
And woman came   at first the tribe had
No word for *years*   but they adapted
The word that once had meant *unending*

1a. How Things in the Garden Ended Before Time Came

They passed the fruit from mouth to mouth
One mouth to the next mouth until
Each person bit the fruit and sang
The lastborn first the firstborn last

One mouth to the next mouth until
The song became a long high scream
The lastborn first the firstborn last
Forgot the song had been a song

The song became a long high scream
Even those who had only sung

Forgot the song had been a song
They forgot even what songs were

Even those who had only sung
Those who had sung the song in words
They forgot even what songs were
They had no words had never had

Those who had sung the song in words
Had sung as the fruit was consumed
They had no words had never had
When instantly the fruit grew back

The Reformation

1.

In the morning what I took
To be the morning   light
Burned through the ceiling sun-
light through a magnifying

Glass through paper but
It looked like a film melt-
ing a   consuming hole
The robot bird flew down

From the ceiling   landed on
My head bent   its head down
And whispered in my ear
Wake up you   fucker all

Night I had stood awake   un-
able to move all night but
As soon as the bird spoke I
Collapsed   the robot hovered

Where my head had been
And barked *Hurry   the fuck*

Up follow me   and turned and
Flew toward a fissure wid-

ening in the fleshy wall
At first it flew in silence
In front of and above me
Guiding me through a narrow

Tall cave   but after we e-
merged into a large chamber
The robot bird transformed
Like Starscream   really like

Any Decepticon
Any Transformer really
Except without the whirring
Into a giant human-

oid robot well   at least
A really tall one eight
Feet tall   at least and gray and
Its arms and legs were thin

As pencils slivers of
What looked like bone   white bone
Jutted from its knuckles
Gray like the parts of cars

You're not supposed to see
Stained with old blood   that rust   red
Color except it's oily
You sometimes see in splotches

On new car parts   in splotches
On the robot too   and stood still
Beside me for a moment
Facing a wide dark pit

In the middle of the chamber
Like an Olympic diver
Standing at the edge of the board
Her gaze fixed neither on

The pool nor any object
In the arena but
Inward instead her eyes
Now signs   now metaphors

Of and for visions no
Spectator could imagine
Before she leaps and leaping
Both transcends and makes

More definite the lim-
its of the human body

And then the robot growled
First stop is processing

Down at the bottom of The-
Pit-You-Can't-See-The-Bottom-
Of is a mountain   we'll
Fall down to the base   then climb

Up to the peak   from there
We'll take an elevator
Down to the center of
The mountain that's   the HR

Bunker the boss wants   if
The boss's boss ever shuts
Us down   to have a record
He wants some evidence that

It was wrong to open Hell and
It's wrong to shut it down
He knows he'll stand before
A judge someday   he needs a

Talented HR team
At this the robot turned
To look me in the eyes
And I think saw my pit-

ying confusion   since as
It stepped to the black edge
Of the pit it   barked *Fuck you*
You think you know what suffer-

ing is   you asshole if
I asked you what it was
You'd probably try to tell me
That's how I know you don't

Know shit   and then it dove
Into the pit and though
I had   followed the bird
Freely I hadn't been

Bound   after it had fallen
Maybe twenty feet
I felt a cord I couldn't
See   unraveling

Before me then I felt
A jolt and a hot sting
As the cord jerked me forward
Too hard and quickly and

Tore through me just above
My hips   I saw my legs

Fall then I realized
The rest of me was falling

After them and falling
Faster than they were
And I flipped upside down
And stretched   forward to catch them

And caught them by my belt
And gasping flipped myself
Right-side up again
And held   my legs beneath

Me by my belt blood sticking
My hands to the belt   as I
Fell   thinking only   were
The buttons on my shirt lined

Up with my zipper   straining
To get a good look shiver-
ing shouting   down to the robot
Buttons   screaming   *Zipper*

2.

I landed on my feet my femurs
Snapped free at the hip   and exited

My body through my upper chest
One on each side and just below my
Shoulders each trailing innards streamers

Burst from a party popper the
Torments of Hell   setting aside
The screams and all that always were
A little bit   funny to see
Like torments in a cartoon fun-

ny and the more   torments I suffered
The funnier the suffering
Of others got but   not till after
A dozen years or so did finding
The suffering of others funny

Become so funny it became
A source of suffering to me
So that was later   *now* I watched
My femurs rocket forward as
The rest of my bones liquefied   my

Eyes sinking in a puddle of
Myself   the right   femur I think the
Right one flew maybe   thirty feet
Before it thudded wetly into
The dirt the left (I had been left-

Handed in life) had   slammed against
The back of the robot's neck   and stuck
A moment then slid wetly down
And touched the black   dirt the same in-
stant the right femur touched it *What*

The fuck the giant   robot barked as
It turned   rubbing its neck   to me
Asshole   that's gonna leave a mark as
It barked I felt a tightening
I knew   was the invisible

Cord I had felt   at the edge of the pit
Even though I had no body it
Constricted my   puddle the way a
Drain constricts water   and I saw
My femurs flying back to me

And felt my insides hardening
And realized I was watching from
A head again   as I watched my
Femurs re-enter me through the holes in
My chest   they had made exiting

The coming back   together was
Agony greater than   the flying
Apart had been   and coming back

Together the   each part   the pro-
cess of it raised me to my feet

Even as my feet   were recon-
stituted   I flew into me
And even though I felt my bones
Straighten inside me even though
I saw my torso and legs merge

And saw my body   still the sound
Of my   body reforming sound-
ed like paint splattering inside me
As if my body   world in world
Were only chaos flung on bones

In Which the Beginning of Time
Happens in a Different Way

In the first days of the Earth
                         before the woman
And man before   time stretched away from the garden
Still clinging to the garden at one end
Like taffy stretched   until it breaks and then
The slow surprise of the taffy's slow collapse
At either edge of the void between its halves
Like half a frown at either of its edges
Before time stretched and broke   and the half clinging
To the garden trapped the garden in the past
A honeybee in honey-golden amber   in the days
That weren't yet days   before the man
Choking on the fat seeds coughed   time   that had been
Hidden in the seeds   into the garden and time filled
The garden and then   after God expelled
The couple   stretched and broke   and one half fol-
lowed them a   dog that eats its master's corpse
In the last days   days that had been before
The woman pounded the man's back   and
He coughed the seeds on the porous black and
Immediately hungry earth   in the last days
That had before time been a single day

Before the hole   between days opened and
Night became as different
From day   as sea is different from land
Although the tribe of Eden never saw or heard the sea
Would never   when the land seemed endless endlessly
Before the day when first a day
Was made of day and night and night   unmade the day
Before the single day began to be unmade the
Darkness the people of the tribe of Eden
Saw when they closed their eyes   they saw
Nowhere in the world   no shadow trav-
eled from the light it bordered   but the darkness they
Saw in themselves was darker than   shadows   and had no
    boundaries
And after the   man and the woman were
Expelled   the people saw the darkness everywhere
They saw it on the now black walls
Now   risen through the clouds   trapping them all
In the garden   and on the skins of the rotten fruit
Fallen from the dead plants they   saw it in the first night
And in the hole that opened
In the trunk of the tree from which the man had eaten
The hole in the tree   grew wider every day
Even as the people grew
Thinner   they watched the darkness in
The hole expand   until they couldn't any-
more believe it   was contained by the tree

Although the people of the tribe could see
The trunk had grown no bigger the
Darkness inside it   had no boundaries
And as they starved some thought the hole was feeding them
In the end the last   of the tribe a   man who had grown thin
And small as a small boy   climbed in

Squeezed in the tree he felt the darkness harden
So began time in the garden

The Dream at the End of the Dream

At the end of the dream the light exploded
The robot   bird the pieces of
The robot flew   each piece about
20   or maybe 25
Feet away burning each piece flew
Then stopped   stalled but I might have said
Froze but the stillness that arrested
The pieces of the robot's body
Was more an engine stopping all
Connected motion   stopping than
A river freezing and the river
Still moves beneath the stillness where
The water meets the air   each burning
Piece flew   then stopped   stalled for an instant
In the air   and for that instant seen
Together   they had flown in all
Directions each   piece the same distance
From the bird as every   other seen to-
gether they formed a sphere around
The hovering   flame where the bird had
Been formed a halo formed a Hum-
vee formed   a cage the burning pieces
Of the bird's exploded body   stalled for

An instant then   the pieces flew
Together back   to the hovering
Flame   and the bird was there again

At the end of the dream the dream continued
And in the dream the robot coughed
Then shook its head   then blinked   once   twice
A third time then it stilled its eyes
On mine   and then it ran to me ran
Past me   behind me   then it shoved
Me   toward a giant camera
Obscura at the edge of the peak
Of the mountain   through the door and toward
The giant aperture in the wall
Opposite the door   through which
I saw a sky beyond the sky
I had   watched all my years on the mountain
And saw a second mountain floating
In the restless sky   high above mine
Which after the bird barked *Hey fuckface*
What do you see I   realized was
The surface of the lake   that was
The gate to Hell   and on the higher
Mountain   above the lake I saw
Through the distorting water saw
Snow at the peak   the farthest snow on
Far mountains   and below it closer

To me the impossibly close stone and
The closer trees   and the trees seemed
To pull me   to the foot of the mountain
My eyes to the foot of the mountain my
Mind in the camera with my body
But also with my eyes   at the foot
Of the mountain   on the mountain's slope
Green grass grew   on the mountain's slope
And small white flowers with petaled stems and
Corollas made of thorns gray moths
The size of with   their wings extended
The size of dimes flew   drunkenly
From flower to flower   on the mountain's slope
Nearest the foot of the mountain   white
Snow   gray stone   green trees the colors
Of the face of the distant mountain close and
Small where the mountain met the dirt
I watched the gray moths stagger from
The petals and the thorns and as
I watched as time   as time before
Had slid from me began to slide
From me at   first I didn't hear it
But once I did   in the midst of the sound I
Realized I'd heard but hadn't noticed
The voice of the bird   filling the sky
Above the mountain filling the
Featureless plain   at the foot of the mountain

Howling a long   approaching *Loooooooooooook*
UP you can't sleep   forever you
Can't dream forever sooner or
Later the dream will wake   and find
You sleeping in its yawning mouth you
Fucker I brought you here   to take you
Away from here   but first you gotta
Look and I looked   and saw myself
High on the mountain climbing and
The bird behind me flying and
Wherever I stepped   the ground wherever
I stepped   after I had stepped two or
Three steps away a piece of the mountain
Broke from the mountainside and flew
Into the sky   and sometimes I
Glanced back to watch a piece of the mountain
Rise but always I turned back
Quickly to face the peak   until
Finally I glancing back I saw a
Black void had opened up behind me
That watching from the foot of the mountain
I long before had seen   I saw
Me finally seeing it and saw
Me finally seeing   that the pieces
Of the mountain each   piece was about the
Size of a Honda Civic had
Arranged themselves   into a wheel

They looked together like a Ferris
Wheel but with no spokes   no hub
And the wheel turned around the axle
Of the line between the darkness of
The void and the   light of the day
The pieces of the mountain rolled
As the wheel turned   into the void one
By one   and disappeared   and as the
Wheel turned the pieces of the mountain
Emerged from the void one by one
And alternately burning or
Encased in ice   and burning or
Encased in ice each rolled to the apex
Of the turning wheel   and at the apex
Of the wheel instantly the flames
Died or the ice   shattered and fell
Away and each   piece of the mountain
Rolled with the wheel back down   I stood
I don't   know for how long I stood there
Watching the wheel   eventually I
Noticed the bird standing beside me
And listening from the foot of the mountain
I heard as if I stood beside
Us I said *What   the fuck is that*
And the bird   who now spoke as it
Had never spoken speaking not
Barking said *The   fire and ice*

Are you and I   and I and you
And each is each   we are the same
Rock burning and we freeze together
And burn and freeze beside each other
Separately also   neither when
We rise together nor when we
Fall separately do we know
Each other   neither in our sorrow
Burning   freezing   nor in our
Joy when we reach the peak and are
Released to joy   and so we burn
And freeze   together on a wheel
That's Hell   you've been in Hell   when I
Was told to guide you through I wasn't
Told where to stop   I realized
I've lived in Hell from the beginning
Of Hell and don't know where it ends
I've never been   given the freedom
To know   and so I thought we'd go
As far as I could go the both
Of us would go as one   as far
As one   and now I think I can't
Go farther we're   at the end   but look at
Me   you are what we are together
And though I watched from the foot of the mountain
As soon as the bird finished speaking
I saw as if I stood before it

I saw the bird transform   a bright

Silvery liquid metal rose

From the bird's joints and coated it

And as the metal thickened the

Bird changed the bird   transformed but not

Into a giant robot but

A person   but a silver person

Silvery like a mirror like

The T-1000   the same height

As me   and with my build and face but

Its features blurred together in

The mirror that made its features and

I only recognized my face

When our two faces were aligned

And otherwise I saw the bird

I mean   I saw myself and knew

It was the bird I saw   and watching

I saw   in its bright skin the mountain

Change shape   at first I thought the change was

The strengthening wind   carving the snowdrifts

But soon I realized the mountain-

side was moving   carrying

The bird and me to the peak I watched

The sky approach in the bird's skin

That was my skin   I watched the sunlight

Open as the light opens in

Movies when the gates of Heaven

Open and the light flooded over

The bird's bright shoulders and bright back
I watched the once-   steep incline gentle
As flowering   trees apple cherry
And lilac trees green   shrubs green grass
And a blue   narrow two   feet wide
A playing stream   appeared in the skin
That was my skin the trees and stream
Warping together and apart
As the bird swayed as we were carried
By the mountainside   and finally
I watched the mountain slow and stop and
I turned from the bird   to see the peak
And saw what I had seen in the bird's
Bright curving skin   but differently
Each thing in its own place and shape
Reflecting sunlight   casting shadows
Echoing from its place forever
Into the earth and heavens like
A hand between two mirrors   facing
Each other a bare empty hand
Alive between infinities
Each thing in its own shape the place and
Sun of an echo of the place and
Shade of the fading echo I
Saw on the green peak

                    but almost as
Soon as I saw the peak I felt

Myself   pulling myself away
From the peak   I fell away from the peak
I fell

     and turned my head away
From the aperture I turned around
To tell the bird what I had seen
And saw the peak   glowing on the door
Opposite the aperture
But upside down I squinted   then
I would have shouted but   the robot
Bird clamped its beak   over my mouth
And nose and rising over me
Its back to the aperture began
Flapping its wings   so rapidly
I thought its wings would break   and flew
Backward through the aperture
Lifting me out of   Hell and into
The cold lake from the bottom of
The lake   out through a film a little
Like it looked   a little like
Brown plastic wrap but passing through
It felt like passing through a fog
Like when you're driving   home in fog
And feel like   you have never known
Your way in the most familiar part
Of the world you know   into the lake

The bird   rising still pulling me
Up through the lake even as the currents
Its wings made pushed me down its wings
Twisting to slice the water as the
Bird lifted them   then flattening
To push the water down and lift
Us both the robot lifted us
Out of the lake   into the world
Into the now   dark sky   the bird's beak
Over my mouth we   crossed the sky
Where I looked and saw the stars